RUGBY F⬤CUS

THE RUGBY WORLD CUP 2015

Sean Callery

WAYLAND

First published in 2015 by Wayland
Copyright © Wayland 2015

Wayland
Hachette Children's Books
338 Euston Road
London NW1 3BH

Wayland Australia
Level 17/207 Kent Street
Sydney, NSW 2000

Produced by White-Thomson Publishing Ltd
White-Thomson Publishing Ltd
www.wtpub.co.uk
+44 (0) 843 208 7460

Editor: Izzi Howell
Designer: Clare Nicholas
Wayland Editor: Annabel Stones

A catalogue for this title is available from the British Library

ISBN: 978 0 7502 9387 7
eBook ISBN: 978 0 7502 9390 7

Dewey Number: 796.3'3365-dc23

10 9 8 7 6 5 4 3 2 1

Wayland is a division of Hachette Children's Books,
an Hachette UK company.
www.hachette.co.uk

The website addresses (URLs) included in this book were valid at the time of going to press.
However, because of the nature of the Internet, it is possible that some addresses may have
changed, or sites may have changed or closed down since publication. While the author
and publisher regret any inconvenience this may cause the readers, no responsibility for
any such changes can be accepted by either the author or the publisher.

Contents

World beater

In autumn 2015, England hosts the biggest rugby festival ever: the Rugby World Cup. Nearly 3 million spectators will cheer 20 teams battling for the top prize in the sport, the Webb Ellis Cup. They will be joined by a massive global TV audience, making the event one of the top sporting competitions in the world.

▲ Joy on the faces of the New Zealand team as they celebrate their 2011 win.

Biggest yet

The Rugby World Cup began in 1987 and is held every four years, each time in a different country. This is the second occasion it has come to the UK. It's a major international contest where the 12 top rugby-playing nations qualify automatically, and another 84 countries compete for the remaining eight spaces. On 18 September, the whistle will blow to kick off the first of 48 matches. Six weeks later, the winners will be decided at the final on 31 October.

CUP FACTS
Previous tournaments

Year	Host	Winner
2011	New Zealand	New Zealand
2007	France	South Africa
2003	Australia	England
1999	Wales	Australia
1995	South Africa	South Africa
1991	England, France, Ireland, Scotland, Wales	Australia
1987	Australia and New Zealand	New Zealand

Sporting chance

The tournament will answer a few of these questions:

- Can trophy holders New Zealand be the first team to win it twice in a row?
- As the home nation, will England reach the final as they did in 1991, 2003 and 2007?
- Can any of the other home nations – Ireland, Scotland and Wales – get beyond the semi-finals for the first time?
- Will any team beat the record number of 22 **tries** scored by Australia against Namibia in 2003?
- Who might add their name to the line-up of six players who have won the World Cup twice?
- Can France end their record of reaching the final three times without winning?

▼ England (in white) and Ireland (in green) show their power and skill contesting a line-out in a warm-up game for the 2011 contest.

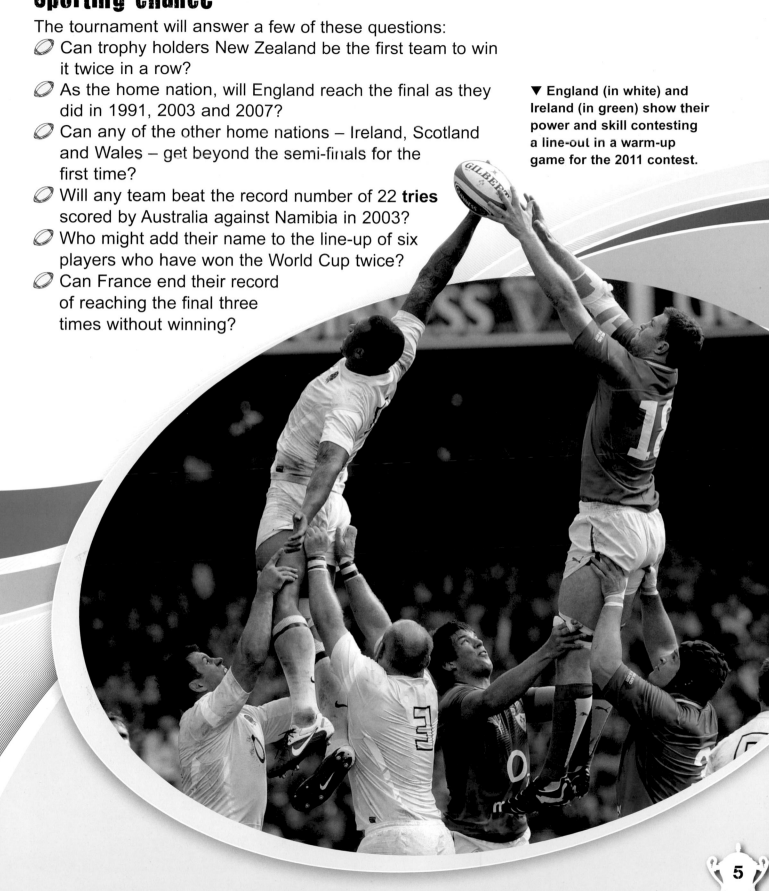

Rugby showpiece

The Rugby World Cup is run by the International Rugby Board (IRB), an organization made up of 118 members from rugby-playing nations. It was founded in 1886.

The IRB decides which country will host the event, choosing locations where the sport is popular, or where there is potential for it to grow. The last World Cup was held in rugby-mad New Zealand. After England 2015, the next tournament will be held in Japan, where the IRB wants to build on the growing Asian interest in the game.

The trophy

The winners' trophy is the Webb Ellis Cup. This is named after William Webb Ellis, who is often said to have invented rugby. In 1823, while a pupil at Rugby School in England, he was playing in a game of football when he caught the ball and ran with it. The game is supposed to have been born in that moment! To promote England 2015, the IRB sent the famous cup on a 15-country global tour, starting with Japan in May 2014.

◄ Standing 38 cm tall, the Webb Ellis Cup weighs 4.5 kg and is made of gilded silver.

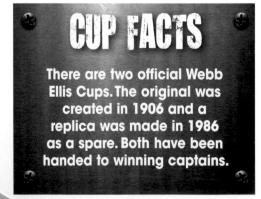

CUP FACTS

There are two official Webb Ellis Cups. The original was created in 1906 and a replica was made in 1986 as a spare. Both have been handed to winning captains.

Big money

The most profitable tournament so far was that hosted by France in 2007, which raised £122.4 million. The IRB expects the 2015 event to beat that and earn £150 million.

The money comes from ticket sales, sponsorship by companies keen to link their name with such a high-profile event, plus money from TV companies. Matches in 2011 were beamed to 207 countries, including, for the first time, the USA. The IRB is keen that TV screens in Asia and North Africa show the tournament, as it is trying to promote the sport in these territories.

▼ Lights are used to transform City Hall in London into a giant rugby ball to advertise the 2015 Rugby World Cup to a wider audience.

RUGBY TALK

Brett Gosper, chief executive of the IRB says:

"We believe it is all shaping up to be a record breaking World Cup."

Keen to host

After the 2011 tournament, a record number of ten nations said they were interested in hosting one of the next two Rugby World Cups. England, Japan, South Africa and Italy put in official bids and England was chosen for 2015, Japan for 2019.

England has promised to hand over £80 million to the IRB in return for hosting the World Cup. It must sell about 2.9 million tickets to raise that sum. With ticket prices ranging from £7 to over £700, the pressure is on!

Host benefits

The benefits of hosting such a big event go beyond the sport. In 2015, about half a million people will visit England and Wales to watch the tournament, and they will spend time and money at other attractions on the days between matches. One estimate says that this, plus money handed over by home supporters, will be worth £1.2 billion to the economy.

CUP FACTS

New Zealand were both host and winner of the first Rugby World Cup in 1987. They defeated France 29-9.

▼ Visitors like these fans at the third-place **play-off** match in New Zealand, 2011, are worth big money to the host country.

▶ Australia's Will Genia meets fans as he arrives in New Zealand for the 2011 tournament.

Seat space

Host countries must have at least one stadium that holds 60,000 people, suitable for the World Cup Final. They also need to offer plenty of venues with top facilities spread around the country so that people don't have to travel too far to see a match.

Team bases

Teams have a base, which may change with each match. Each base must have:

- A hotel
- An outdoor training area
- An indoor training area
- A gym
- A swimming pool

In previous World Cups, teams have made friends with the community where they are based, and gained plenty of fans to cheer them on, adding extra atmosphere at matches.

CUP FACTS

One reason for a country to host the World Cup is that they stand a better chance of winning when supported by their home crowd. The host team has won three tournaments out of seven!

England at home

England shared the hosting of the 1991 tournament with France, Ireland, Scotland and Wales. They managed to reach the final, where they lost 12–6 to Australia. This time the only matches outside the country will be in Wales.

Decade of sport

The Rugby World Cup will be a major UK sports event in 2015, and is part of a 'Decade of Sport' in England. Other major events in this period include the Olympics (2012), the Rugby League World Cup (2013), the first stages of the Tour de France (2014), the World Athletics Championship (2017) and the Cricket World Cup (2019).

Where are we going?

The organizers have chosen stadiums across England (plus one in Wales) to give as many people as possible the chance to see a match. They have also chosen to hold some matches at football stadiums whose larger capacities will bring games to the widest possible audience.

RUGBY TALK

England Rugby 2015 chief executive Debbie Jevans says of the stadiums chosen:

"It is a great mix and will ensure that 92% of the population is within 50 miles of a World Cup venue."

▼ Five matches will be played at London's Olympic Stadium, where the spectacular opening ceremony of the 2012 Olympics took place.

Stadium locations

Venue	Location	Capacity	Matches to be hosted	Stadium type	Map ref
Twickenham	London	81,605	10	Rugby	1
Wembley	London	90,256	2	Football	2
Olympic Stadium	London	54,000	5	Multi sport	3
Millennium Stadium	Cardiff, Wales	74,154	8	Rugby	4
City of Manchester Stadium	Manchester	47,800	1	Football	5
St James' Park	Newcastle	52,409	3	Football	6
Elland Road	Leeds	37,914	2	Football	7
King Power Stadium	Leicester	32,312	3	Football	8
Villa Park	Birmingham	42,785	2	Football	9
Kingsholm Stadium	Gloucester	16,115	4	Rugby	10
Stadium mk	Milton Keynes	30,717	3	Football	11
Brighton Community Stadium	Brighton	30,750	2	Football	12
Sandy Park	Exeter	12,300	3	Rugby	13

The race for a place

There are twenty places available for teams in the Rugby World Cup. The twelve top teams (decided by the IRB according to their recent results) get automatic places. For 2015 these are New Zealand, South Africa, Australia, England, Ireland, Wales, France, Scotland, Samoa, Italy, Tonga and Argentina.

Shared opportunity

That leaves eight places up for grabs. These are awarded through the **qualification** process, which this time saw 84 teams take part in 203 matches. Teams from Europe and the Americas get two places each, while Asia, Africa and Oceania get one each. The runners-up from those contests have a chance to win the last place in a final series of matches called the **repechage**.

Chances taken

Europe saw 31 teams compete, with Georgia and Romania winning out. From the 18-strong field in the Americas, Canada took the first place, with the USA managing to grab the second spot by beating Uruguay. Fiji swept aside the Cook Islands 108–6 to take the Oceania spot, while Japan convincingly beat Hong Kong 49–8 to win the Asia Five Nations and a World Cup place.

▼ Georgia (in white) beat Romania 25–9 at the 2011 World Cup. Both teams made it through the qualifiers for the 2015 tournament.

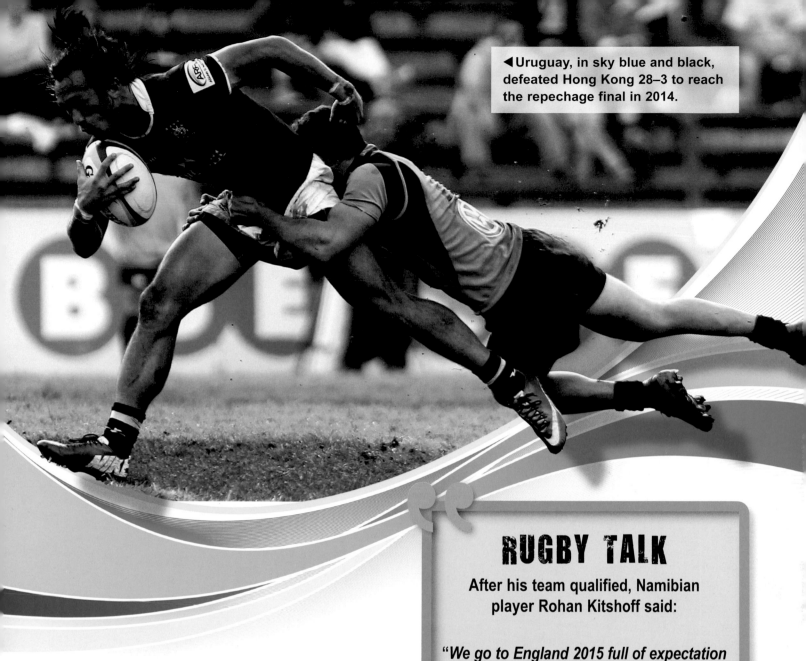

RUGBY TALK

After his team qualified, Namibian player Rohan Kitshoff said:

"We go to England 2015 full of expectation and are determined to do ourselves, our nation and African rugby proud."

Last-minute winners

Africa saw a dramatic finish. On the last day of qualifying, Kenya were favourites, but they lost to Zimbabwe, putting Zimbabwe through to the repechage play-off. Namibia needed to beat Madagascar to stand a chance of qualifying. The team rose to the challenge and won 89–10. Their **points difference** of +76 earned them the final place in the 2015 Rugby World Cup pool stage.

The repechage

Russia, Hong Kong, Zimbabwe and Uruguay went into the repechage. Russia and Uruguay got the better of Hong Kong and Zimbabwe and met for a two-match decider. The first game left Russia just ahead but Uruguay fought back to take the final place in the 2015 Rugby World Cup by 57–49 overall.

The showdown

The World Cup tournament is split into two stages. First, groups of five teams play each other in the pool stage. The top eight teams go through to the knockout stage that ends with the final decider.

The pool stage

The 20 teams are divided into four groups in a system that aims to keep the best apart until the knockout stage. The four nations with the highest rankings in December 2012 were put in pools A to D, as Band 1. Then came the next eight highest ranking teams in Bands 2 and 3. The last two places in each pool went to qualifiers. The pools for 2015 are:

	Pool A	Pool B	Pool C	Pool D
Band 1	Australia	South Africa	New Zealand	France
Band 2	England	Samoa	Argentina	Ireland
Band 3	Wales	Scotland	Tonga	Italy
Qualifiers	Fiji	Japan	Georgia	Canada
	Uruguay	USA	Namibia	Romania

Scoring System

Basic points:
Win=4 points, Draw=2 points

Bonus points:
Scoring four tries or more=1 point,
Losing by seven points or fewer=1 point

Maximum points per game: 5

The knockout stage

The top two teams in each pool go to the next round, the quarter-finals. The winners progress to the semi-finals and then the final, with third and fourth places decided by one last match.

Each game is won by the team that scores the most points, with 20 minutes of extra time being played if the score is level. If it's still a draw, the match goes to 'sudden death' – this only lasts ten minutes and whoever scores first, wins. If the score is still level, a winner is decided through a penalty kicking contest, although this has not happened at a Rugby World Cup yet. Then, at last, the winners lift the trophy!

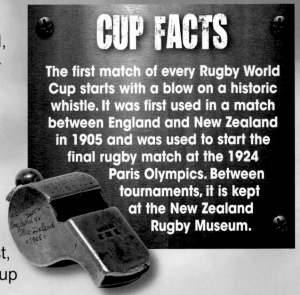

CUP FACTS

The first match of every Rugby World Cup starts with a blow on a historic whistle. It was first used in a match between England and New Zealand in 1905 and was used to start the final rugby match at the 1924 Paris Olympics. Between tournaments, it is kept at the New Zealand Rugby Museum.

Quarter-Final 1

Sat 17 October, 16:00
Venue: Twickenham Stadium

Winner Pool B *vs* Runner-Up Pool A

Quarter-Final 2

Sat 17 October, 20:00
Venue: Millennium Stadium

Winner Pool C *vs* Runner-Up Pool D

Quarter-Final 3

Winner Pool D *vs* Runner-Up Pool C

Quarter-Final 4

Winner Pool A *vs* Runner-Up Pool B

Semi-Final 1

Sat 24 October, 16:00
Venue: Twickenham Stadium

Winner QF1 *vs* Winner QF2

Semi-Final 2

Sun 25 October, 16:00
Venue: Twickenham Stadium

Winner QF3 *vs* Winner QF4

Third place play-off

Friday 30 October, 20:00
Venue: Olympic Stadium

Runner-Up SF1 *vs* Runner-Up SF2

Final

Saturday 31 October, 16:00
Venue: Twickenham Stadium

Winner SF1 *vs* Winner SF2

Squad power

There are 15 players on the pitch per game, but twice that many make up each squad. A supporting cast of coaches, medical staff and organizers is waiting off the pitch to make sure the team is ready and in good shape for every match.

Team blend

Each squad has 30 players. The selection usually includes more **forwards** than **backs** because of the need to have enough players who are experienced in the **scrum**. It will also include more than one specialist **kicker**, in case one of them is injured or doesn't play as well as expected.

Managers often go for a blend of experienced players who know what it feels like to play in major tournaments, and younger players keen to make a name for themselves at the top level. From the squad, they select 22 players who can be used in each match, including seven substitutes on the bench.

CUP FACTS

John Kirwan played 11 Rugby World Cup matches for New Zealand, and has since been involved in four as a coach for Italy, and eight as a coach for Japan. His total of 23 RWC matches is a record.

▼ French players recover on the substitutes' bench as their fresh replacements continue the battle on the pitch.

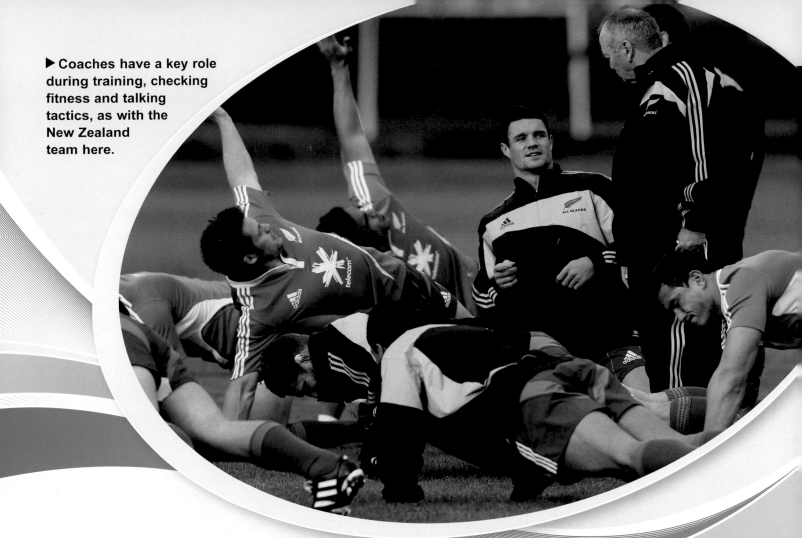

▶ Coaches have a key role during training, checking fitness and talking tactics, as with the New Zealand team here.

The team behind the team

The backroom team is vital for success. It includes a manager, several coaches, and other supporting roles. Coaches have special responsibilities: some will work mainly with the forwards on specialist areas, such as **line-outs**. Others will work with the defence. There is often one to keep a check on fitness, helping players recover from the last match and prepare for the next one. Other coaches specialize in mental preparation: being in the right state of mind for the match.

Supporting roles include people in charge of fuelling the team with the right food and drink, medical staff to deal with injuries, and travel support staff who make sure the squad are moved safely and efficiently between training bases and match venues.

TOUCHDOWN

Players cover about 7 km in every match, and may be involved in 300 'impacts' such as **tackles, rucks, mauls** and collisions. They'll lose about 2 litres of fluid from their body in sweat. Support staff help them train to cope with this and recover to do it again a few days later.

Teams from Africa and Asia

The two African teams to have qualified come from the same continent, but they are worlds apart. South Africa is a giant of the sport, while Namibia is yet to win a World Cup game. Japan has been Asia's top rugby side for many years and will host the 2019 World Cup.

South Africa

With its record of two wins in two finals, South Africa is a threat to any team. They are currently ranked second in the world by the IRB, and stand a real chance of winning the 2015 World Cup.

◄ Rugby helped to unite a new nation in 1995 when President Nelson Mandela congratulated Francois Pienaar after South Africa's World Cup win.

Colours	Green and white
Nickname	Springboks, after an African antelope
World Cups	All since 1995
Best result	1995 win that united a new nation
Worst result	29–9 loss to New Zealand in the 2003 quarter finals
Key players	Marcell Coetzee, Duane Vermeulen, Handré Pollard

18

▶ Namibia's Jacques Burger takes on the Welsh defence during the 2011 tournament.

Namibia

Namibia has played 15 matches in World Cup tournaments, and lost all of them, sometimes by a huge number of points.

Colours	Blue and white
Nickname	Welwitschias, from a plant that features on the country's coat of arms
World Cups	All since 1999
Best result	Great fight back against Ireland in 2007, but they still lost 32–17
Worst result	142–0 hammering by Australia in 2003
Key players	Jacques Burger, PJ van Lill

Japan

Japan has a fast style of play that produces great tries, but struggles against the sheer physical power of opponents at this level.

Colours	Red, black and white
Nickname	Brave Blossoms, Cherry Blossoms
World Cups	All
Best result	1991 win over Zimbabwe, their only win
Worst result	145–17 mauling by New Zealand in 1995
Key players	Michael Leitch, Atsushi Hiwasa, Ayumu Goromaru

19

Teams from the Americas

Rugby is becoming more popular in the Americas, although it faces tough competition from other sports. Only Argentina qualified automatically.

 ## Argentina

Argentina has reached the knockout stages of the last two World Cups, each time losing to the eventual winners.

Colours	Sky blue and white
Nickname	Los Pumas – even though the cat on their badge is a jaguar, not a puma
World Cups	All
Best result	Beating France 34–10 to take third place in 2007
Worst result	Losing all their pool games in 1991 and 1995
Key players	Agustín Creevy, Juan Martín Fernández Lobbe

 ## Uruguay

Uruguay won a game in each of their previous World Cups, against Spain in 1999 and Georgia in 2003. They narrowly failed to qualify in 2007 and 2011.

Colours	Black and blue
Nickname	Los Teros, a South American bird
World Cups	1999, 2003
Best result	Beating Georgia 24–12 in 2003
Worst result	Getting beaten 111–13 by England in 2003
Key players	Nicolás Klappenbach, Felipe Berchesi

ONE TO WATCH

Hooker Agustín Creevy is a natural leader with great ball-handling skills who played in all five of The Pumas' games in the last World Cup.

Canada

Canada has reached the knockout stages once in 1991, and managed a draw and a win in the pool stage last time round.

Colours	Red, white and black
Nickname	Maple Leafs, after the Canadian national emblem
World Cups	All
Best result	Reaching the quarter finals in 1991
Worst result	Finishing bottom of their pool in 2007 without a win
Key players	Tyler Ardron, James Pritchard

▶ **Phil Mack in the red of Canada looks for a killer pass against the USA during their repechage match.**

USA

The USA team will be hoping to improve on its record of only three wins in 21 World Cup matches.

Colours	Blue and white
Nickname	Eagles, after the national bird of the USA
World Cups	All except 1995
Best result	Beating Japan 39–26 in 2003, the most points they have ever scored
Worst result	Losing 25–15 to Tonga in 2007, when they were favourites to win
Key players	Todd Clever, Blaine Scully

UK and Irish teams

These four teams form part of the Six Nations contest along with France and Italy. They struggle to challenge the rugby giants from the southern hemisphere.

England

Three finals with one win makes England the only northern hemisphere side to have held the trophy.

Colours	White
Nickname	None
World Cups	All
Best result	Won in 2003, beating Australia in the last seconds by 20–17
Worst result	Losing 44–21 to South Africa in the 1999 quarter finals
Key players	Chris Robshaw, Courtney Lawes, Mike Brown

Ireland

Ireland has delivered some thrilling performances in international games – but not often at the World Cup.

Colours	Green and white
Nickname	None
World Cups	All
Best result	Beating Australia in 2011 by 15–6
Worst result	1999 loss to Argentina 24–28 in the quarter-final play-offs
Key players	Jonathan Sexton, Seán O'Brien, Rob Kearney

ONE TO WATCH

Flanker Chris Robshaw is more than just a great tackler and ball carrier: he is a leader who inspires his England teammates.

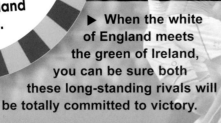

▶ When the white of England meets the green of Ireland, you can be sure both these long-standing rivals will be totally committed to victory.

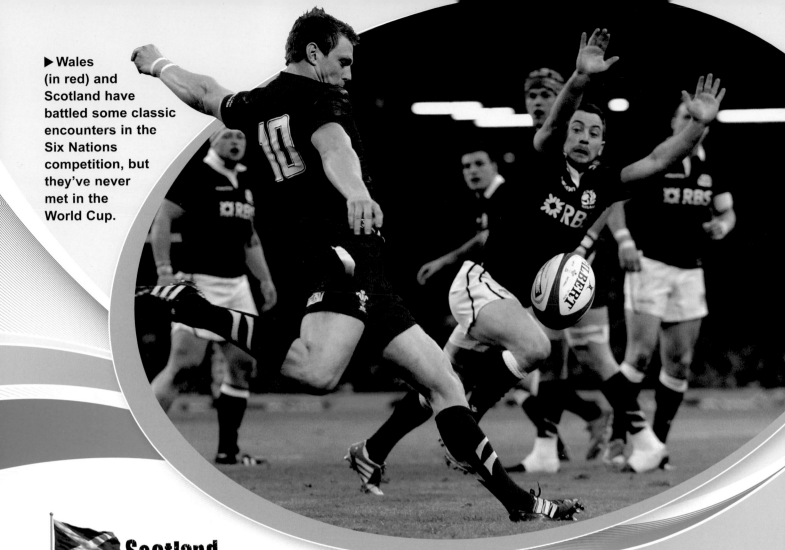

▶ Wales (in red) and Scotland have battled some classic encounters in the Six Nations competition, but they've never met in the World Cup.

Scotland

Scotland missed the knockout stages for the first time in 2011 after four very tight pool matches.

Colours	Blue and white
Nickname	None
World Cups	All
Best result	Finished fourth in 1991
Worst result	Missed the knockout stages in 2011
Key players	Kelly Brown, Stuart Hogg, Richie Gray

Wales

The Dragons came close to the 2011 final, losing 9–8 to France in the semis.

Colours	Red
Nickname	Dragons, because of the Welsh flag
World Cups	All
Best result	Beat Australia 22–21 to get third place in 1987
Worst result	Losing at home 16–13 to Samoa in 1991
Key players	Sam Warburton, Dan Lydiate, George North

European teams: Mainland

Of the other European teams, only France have challenged the rugby giants at the World Cup. Will this be the year that up-and-coming teams, such as Georgia and Romania, finally make their presence felt?

 France

The French side is unpredictable, being capable of brilliance and sloppiness in the same match.

Colours	Blue and red
Nickname	Les bleus, after their kit colour
World Cups	All
Best result	Came very close to winning their 2011 final
Worst result	Lost 19–14 to Tonga in 2011
Key players	Louis Picamoles, Thierry Dusautoir, Wesley Fofana

 **Georgia**

Georgia has reached the tournament for the fourth time in a row.

Colours	Red and white
Nickname	The Lelos. Lelo is a traditional Georgian ball game
World Cups	All
Best result	30–0 against Namibia in 2007, their first World Cup win
Worst result	Losing 24–12 to underdogs Uruguay in 2003
Key players	Irakli Machkhaneli, Mamuka Gorgodze

◀ Louis Picamoles has been a regular for France since 2008. The big, strong number eight is a great carrier of the ball.

Italy

Italy is gaining international experience but has yet to make an impact in the World Cup.

Colours	Blue
Nickname	Azzurri (Sky Blues) after their kit colour
World Cups	All
Best result	A 53–17 victory over Russia in 2011
Worst result	The 1999 humiliation 101–3 by New Zealand
Key players	Sergio Parisse, Michele Campagnaro

 # Romania

Romania has managed just five wins in seven World Cup visits.

Colours	Blue and yellow
Nickname	The Oaks
World Cups	All
Best result	Nearly beat Scotland in 2011
Worst result	90–8 drubbing by Australia in 2003
Key players	Ovidiu Tonita, Mihai Macovei

ONE TO WATCH

Sergio Parisse is one of the top number eights ever – a position for a player who can tackle, run and is always in the thick of the action.

Teams from Oceania

The Pacific region is a hotbed for rugby. It boasts two giants of the game, Australia and New Zealand, and three 'minnows' from tiny islands who manage the occasional giant-kill but usually struggle to get out of the pool stage.

New Zealand

With a population of only 4.5 million, New Zealand is an unlikely rugby world power, but the All Blacks dominate at the moment.

Colours	Black
Nickname	All Blacks, after their kit colour
World Cups	All
Best result	Won in 1987 and 2011
Worst result	Lost to France in the 2007 quarter finals
Key players	Richie McCaw, Julian Savea, Ma'a Nonu

Fiji

A hard-running, tough-tackling side who haven't always qualified for the World Cup.

Colours	Black and white
Nickname	Flying Fijians
World Cups	All except 1995
Best result	Beat Wales 38–34 in 2007 to reach the last eight
Worst result	Steamrollered 66–0 by Wales in 2011
Key players	Akapusi Qera, Vereniki Goneva

▲ The All Blacks perform their haka before every match. This traditional Maori dance includes jumps, stamps, chants and face-pulling.

ONE TO WATCH

Powerfully built Julian Savea scored three tries on his All Blacks debut in 2012 and has continued to scare defences with his speedy wing play.

Australia

Australia was the first nation to lift the trophy twice and came third in the 2011 tournament.

Colours	Green and yellow
Nickname	Wallabies, after a famous Australian animal
World Cups	All
Best result	Won in 1991 and 1999
Worst result	Went out 25–22 to England in the 1995 quarter finals
Key players	Stephen Moore, Michael Hooper, Israel Folau

Samoa

Originally known as Western Samoa, this team is the top performer of the Pacific 'minnows'.

Colours	Blue and white
Nickname	Manu Samoa, after a famous Samoan warrior
World Cups	All since 1991
Best result	Beat Wales 16–13 in 1991 and again 38–31 in 1999
Worst result	Lost 59–7 against South Africa in 2007
Key players	David Lemi, Paul Williams

Tonga

A sensational defeat of France at the last tournament shows this team has giant-killing potential.

Colours	Red and white
Nickname	'Ikale Tahi', which means 'Sea Eagles'
World Cups	All except 1991
Best result	Beat Italy 28–25 in 1999 and France 14–19 in 2011
Worst result	Lost 101–10 to England in 1999
Key players	Nili Latu, Sona Taumalolo

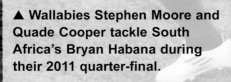
▲ Wallabies Stephen Moore and Quade Cooper tackle South Africa's Bryan Habana during their 2011 quarter-final.

Around the world

The Rugby World Cup is the IRB's major rugby title, but the organization also supports other events to promote and celebrate rugby around the world, including Pacific, Women's, Junior and Sevens competitions.

Women's World Cup

The Women's World Cup began in 1991 and since 1994 has been run every four years. The most recent tournament was hosted by France in 2014. New Zealand were favourites, having won four titles between 1998 and 2010, but they lost to Ireland and didn't make the final! Instead, England beat Canada 21–9 to lift the trophy. The high standard of play in the tournament drew sell-out crowds and record TV audiences, raising the profile of the women's game. Following their World Cup win, 20 of the England women's squad were able to give up their day jobs and take up contracts to play the sport full time.

Junior tournaments

The IRB runs two competitions for national teams with players under 20 years old. The Junior World Championship features the top 12 teams and has been held every year since 2008. The 2014 event was hosted by New Zealand and saw England edge past South Africa 21–20 to win it for the second time. The 2015 tournament will be held in Italy in June, a few months before the seniors battle for the World Cup in England. The Junior World Trophy is for eight smaller teams. In 2014 Japan won it for the first time, earning a place at the next Championship.

RUGBY TALK

England women's captain and fly half, Katy McLean said of their recent win:

"This is fantastic news for the sport and exactly what we need as an England squad to continue to be at the top of our sport on a global scale."

▶ England's Emily Scarratt powers through the Canadian defence during the 2014 Women's World Cup final.

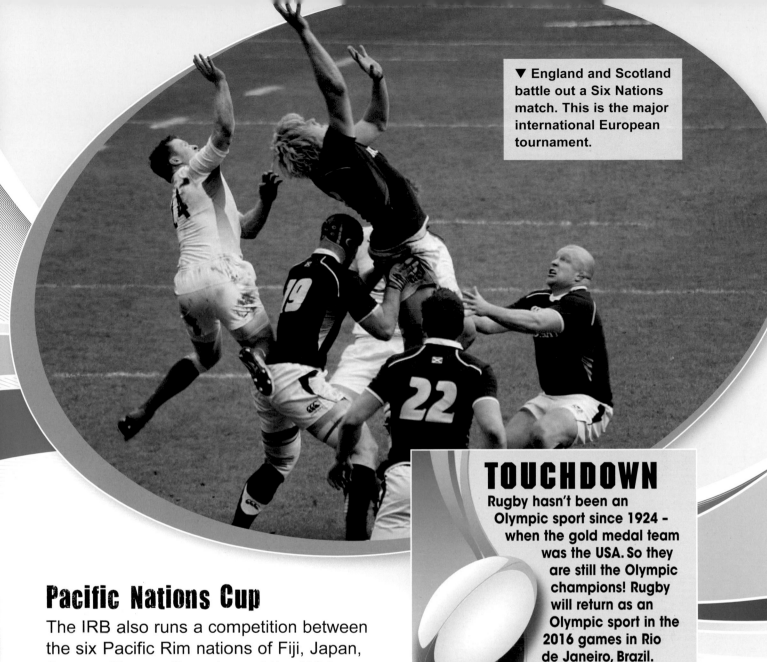

▼ England and Scotland battle out a Six Nations match. This is the major international European tournament.

TOUCHDOWN

Rugby hasn't been an Olympic sport since 1924 – when the gold medal team was the USA. So they are still the Olympic champions! Rugby will return as an Olympic sport in the 2016 games in Rio de Janeiro, Brazil.

Pacific Nations Cup

The IRB also runs a competition between the six Pacific Rim nations of Fiji, Japan, Samoa, Tonga, Canada and the USA. It aims to raise the standard of play by giving players the opportunity to play international rugby.

Non-IRB competitions

The biggest other competitions include the Six Nations Championship, where England, France, Ireland, Italy, Scotland and Wales battle to find the best team in Europe. Argentina, Australia, New Zealand and South Africa's equivalent is The Rugby Championship.

Beyond rugby

The IRB uses its high profile to support the United Nations World Food Programme's Tackle Hunger campaign, which helps people who don't have enough to eat. An estimated 842 million people go hungry every day, most of them in undeveloped parts of Africa and Asia. The scheme helps to feed 97 million people in 80 countries.

The World Cup in numbers

6
Six players have won the World Cup twice: Dan Crowley, John Eales, Tim Horan, Phil Kearns and Jason Little (all for Australia in 1991 and 1999) plus Os du Randt (for South Africa in 1995 and 2007).

39
Gavin Hastings of Scotland kicked a record 39 **conversions** in Rugby World Cup history, two more than New Zealand's Grant Fox.

19
The USA's Thretton Palemo became the youngest ever player at the World Cup in 2007 at the age of 19 years and eight days.

126
No-one has scored more points in a single tournament than Grant Fox of New Zealand, with 126 in 1987.

22
Jason Leonard's 22 appearances for England in World Cup matches from 1991–2003 is a record.

82,957
The biggest crowd was the 82,957 in Sydney who saw Australia lose 17–20 to England in 2003.

1,000
Japan is the only team to have conceded more than 1,000 points so far in all tournaments.

15
Jonah Lomu of New Zealand and Bryan Habana of South Africa share the record of scoring eight tries in one competition, in 1999 and 2007 respectively. Lomu holds the total tries record with 15.

3
Only three World Cup matches have been draws: 20-all between France and Scotland in 1987; then 12-all in 2007 and 23-all in 2001 between Canada and Japan.

45
Simon Culhane scored 45 points for New Zealand against Japan in 1995, a record for one player in a match.

◀ Jonny Wilkinson became a national hero in England when he kicked a goal in the last seconds of extra time to win the World Cup against Australia in 2003. He holds the record for points scored at World Cups: a total of 277.

30

Further information

Glossary

back – a player who lines up behind the forwards and is involved in attacking moves

conversion – a score after a try by kicking the ball over the crossbar

forward – a player who is involved in scrums and line-outs

kicker – the player who kicks conversions and penalties

knockout stage – the part of a competition where only the winner goes to the next round

line-out – restarting play when the forwards form two lines at right angles to the touchline and jump for the ball when it is thrown in

maul – a loose scrum formed around a player with the ball off the ground

play-offs – a series of games to decide an overall winner

points difference – the number of points scored, minus the number of points lost

qualification – getting through to the next round of a competition

repechage – like a play-off, but with teams who missed getting to the next stage by a small amount

ruck – a loose scrum formed around a player with the ball on the ground

scrum – restarting play when players from each team group together and try to get the ball when it is rolled in

tackle – challenging an opposing player who is carrying the ball

try – scoring by placing the ball on the ground behind the opposing team's goal line

Books

Sporting Skills: Rugby
by Clive Gifford (Wayland, 2014)

Rugby Focus series
by Jon Richards (Wayland, 2015)

Know Your Sport: Rugby
by Clive Gifford (Franklin Watts, 2012)

Websites

www.rugbyworldcup.com
The official site for information about World Cups past and present.

www.irb.com
Site of the International Rugby Board, which promotes rugby around the world.

www.bbc.co.uk/sport/0/rugby-union
Has plenty of information on world rugby.

Index

MORE SPORTS TITLES FROM WAYLAND!

Find out more about all sorts of sports with these brilliant titles.

Rugby Focus

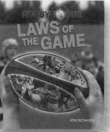

978 0 7502 9479 9
978 0 7502 9481 2
978 0 7502 9480 5

Generation Cricket

978 0 7502 8300 7
978 0 7502 9270 2

Sporting Skills

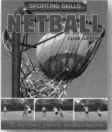

978 0 7502 8119 5
978 0 7502 8120 1
978 0 7502 7865 2
978 0 7502 8118 8

Mad about

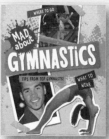

978 0 7502 8268 0
978 0 7502 8270 3
978 0 7502 8271 0

Inspirational lives

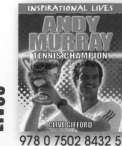

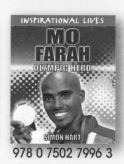

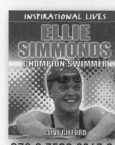

978 0 7502 8432 5
978 0 7502 8358 8
978 0 7502 7996 3
978 0 7502 8367 0
978 0 7502 8359 5